Scripture and Authority Today

Richard Bauckham

Professor of New Testament Studies
University of St Andrews

GROVE BOOKS LIMITED
RIDLEY HALL RD CAMBRIDGE CB3 9HU

Contents

1. Authority—Extrinsic and Intrinsic 3
2. The Modernist Rejection of Authority 5
3. The Postmodernist Rejection of Authority 8
4. The Authority of the Biblical Story 10
5. The Authority of Grace 14
6. Story, Commands and Doctrines 16
7. Other Modes of Authority 19
8. Authority and Freedom in Biblical Interpretation 20
9. Bibliography 24

Note
A shorter version of this essay was published as 'Scripture and Authority,' in *Transformation* 15/2 (1998) pp 5–11.

The Cover Illustration is by Mike Higton

Copyright © Richard Bauckham 1999

First Impression June 1999
ISSN 1365-490X
ISBN 1 85174 405 3

1
Authority — Extrinsic and Intrinsic

A useful distinction with which to begin (because we shall make use of it in what follows) is the distinction between extrinsic and intrinsic authority. If you accept a statement as true, not because the statement in itself can convince you of its truth, but because the person making the statement is qualified to make it, has the authority to say what is true in this case, then the statement depends on authority external to it—extrinsic authority. If you obey a command, not because you can see the point or purpose of what you are being required to do, but because the person making the command has the authority to command you, then the command relies on extrinsic authority. If you are sick and go to a medical doctor, who diagnoses your condition, tells you what is wrong, and prescribes medicine, you may well be quite unable to judge for yourself whether her diagnosis is correct or whether her prescription is likely to work, but because she has medical qualifications and is regarded as reliable by your community, you trust her diagnosis and obey her orders. This is extrinsic authority. If, on the other hand, someone observed that your poor state of health could well be due to the overwork and stress you have been suffering recently and that you really ought to take a holiday, you might find this a convincing diagnosis and be able to see that the advice is sensible. In this case it does not matter who makes the observation; they need no particular expertise or authority to back up their statements. The statement itself convinces you, so that you accept it as true and do what it requires of you. The statement has intrinsic authority.

It is also worth noticing that in many everyday situations extrinsic and intrinsic authority are both operative in varying degrees. Imagine yourself the pupil of an expert teacher, whose authority to speak about his subject is not merely textbook knowledge but is also based on half a lifetime's experience of the subject. He will give you factual knowledge, which you can in fact check for yourself from the books if you feel the need. But you will also benefit from his powers of judgment, his accumulated knowledge of what works in the subject. This you have to trust, though gradually, as you become expert yourself, you will be able to verify such things from your own experience. But finally there may also be personal knowledge which you cannot check or verify for yourself. A teacher of modern art who had known Picasso personally might tell you anecdotes about the artist or report what Picasso had told him about his work. Here you or anyone else could only take his word for it. This does not at all mean that you have to be credulous or uncritical. You may have grounds for trusting your teacher's accounts, because you have been impressed by him as a reliable person. What he tells you may cohere with whatever else you know of Picasso and so be plausible. It may, as it were, ring true. But in the end you take what the teacher says on trust. So in this example there is, in some areas of the knowledge you gain, a shift from more reliance on extrinsic to more reliance on intrinsic authority, as you yourself come to understand the subject more profoundly, but there are also areas in which extrinsic authority is irreplaceable. In a mature understanding of the subject, as much of what you have been taught you come to find convincing in itself, so also your grounds for trusting what you cannot in principle verify become more substantial.

If we apply this kind of analysis of authority to the Bible, it seems to me that for most believers the Bible's authority is a combination of extrinsic and intrinsic elements, and that this is also how the contents of the Bible represent themselves. Surprisingly rarely do the biblical writers demand obedience or belief by sheer appeal to the authority of God. They appeal in all kinds of ways to reason, imagination and experience. They persuade and convince in all the ways in which literature can persuade and convince. Certainly there is a major dimension which can only be taken on trust, but it is constantly admixed with the intrinsic authoritativeness of what is said. Moreover, like the pupil of the expert teacher, it is surely true that much of what Christians must begin by taking simply on trust gains a degree of intrinsic authority for them as they grow more deeply into and practise the faith. (Moreover, we should think of the community of faith here as much as of the individual. The community's experience of the intrinsic authoritativeness of Scripture far surpasses the individual's.) The Bible claims an irreplaceable and important element of extrinsic authority, but it does not rely on this alone.

This seems to me broadly consistent with traditional doctrines of Scripture. Perhaps these have emphasized the extrinsic authority of Scripture too one-sidedly: Scripture has the authority of God's Word and what it says should be believed because God has the authority to say it. But traditionally the inspiration of Scripture had as its corollary the inspiration of the reader of Scripture or the reading community. The Spirit who inspired the Scripture also inspires its believing readers to accept it as God's message and to understand it. This should not be understood as a kind of magic which makes credible to us what would otherwise have no credibility. It can be understood to mean that as the Spirit inspires our Christian living and thinking, leading us further into the experience of what the Bible teaches, so we find the Bible making more sense to us—existentially, intellectually, imaginatively. As the Spirit actualizes the Word of God in our lives, so the Word of God authenticates itself to us.

2
The Modernist Rejection of Authority

Authority is not a concept which has fared well in the modern period. Indeed, I think we have got to the stage in the western cultural context where for many people authority is indistinguishable from authoritarianism. Authority, which was once a good word, has acquired largely negative connotations. So, if we are to understand the dynamics of people's problems with authority and defences of authority within the churches, we need to understand this broader cultural context from which such problems stem. In particular, it is essential to distinguish what I shall call 'modernist' forms of rejection of authority from 'postmodernist' ones. These are significantly different.

I use the term 'modernist' to refer to the characteristic worldview which stems from the European Enlightenment and has spread from Europe to much of the world in some degree. I shall use the term 'postmodernist' to refer to the intellectual and cultural outlook which has recently been superseding modernism in Europe and the United States especially, but not without influence elsewhere. I stress at the outset that the two outlooks overlap. In Europe and America we are in a period of cultural transition, in which modernist attitudes are still influentially present alongside the postmodernist ones. It is not yet clear whether postmodernism will become the enduring successor to modernist culture, but it is at present a strong contender.

The Enlightenment Principle

According to Immanuel Kant, the motto of the Enlightenment is: 'Have the courage to use your own intelligence!' The Enlightenment rejected traditional authorities, both institutional and intellectual, in the name of autonomous reason. What is worthy of belief is what can in principle be established by rational argument by any intelligent person. What is worthy of moral obedience is what can be discerned as the moral imperative by any rational person. Submission to extrinsic authority—believing or acting merely on someone else's say-so—is incompatible with the autonomy of the individual rational person.

It looks as though modernism, therefore, rejects extrinsic authority and affirms intrinsic authority, but it is not quite so simple. With regard to extrinsic authority, the modern world is in practice heavily dependent on the authority of the expert, especially the scientist. The modern project of extending rational control over human life and the rest of the world requires the accumulation of knowledge—indeed, the formation of traditions of knowledge and practice

—which it is impossible for individuals to verify for themselves. Not only the lay person but even a scientist relies on the work of his predecessors and could not practicably verify all of their conclusions for himself. However, they could *in principle* be verified. What modernism rejects is authority that cannot be checked, tested and criticized.

But it is important also to notice that for modernism what counts as the criterion for intrinsic authority is a particular and rather narrow concept of reason. One should be convinced only of what can be demonstrated empirically or from first principles in a way that is universally accessible. Hence, in part, the enormous prestige of natural science as the model of true knowledge in modernism. Hence also the attempt to establish moral values as universally recognizable independently of particular cultural and religious traditions. Enlightenment rationality aims to replace all particular traditions of thought and practice, whose inherited wisdom and insights seem to it to have no rational foundation. Such traditions' complex combinations of extrinsic authority and intrinsic authoritativeness are missed and dismissed, since they do not allow the abstract universal verification which modernism demands.

Modernism and the Bible

So, having specified in what the modernist rejection of authority consists, we may ask how the authority of the Bible fares in encounter with it. The Bible clearly represents a particular tradition of faith, rooted in a particular history and its interpretation. Its truth claims do not seem open to universal verification in accordance with modernist requirements. However, the Bible was too central to European culture to be dismissed as easily as European cultural imperialists dismissed the traditions of their subject peoples. So, about the Bible's encounter with modernist canons of rational belief, I will make three points:

1   Much effort in nineteenth-century biblical studies and theology was devoted to the attempt to reconstruct the Bible's value for Christian faith in a way that escapes the modern rejection of authority. There are two main aspects to this. One is historical criticism in its typical nineteenth- and early twentieth-century form (also still with us, of course), that is, the attempt to get behind the way the Bible interprets the story it tells to 'what really happened'—a purely objective account of the historical facts from which rational modern people may draw their own conclusions. The historical Jesus—reconstructed by critical historical method—replaces the biblical Christ as the basis of Christian faith. Secondly, there is the attempt to understand the message of the Bible as the proclamation of moral values which are universally accessible to reason, but of which the

biblical history is a useful instantiation.

Modernism dies hard, and so these issues are still with us. Witness the continuing popularity of pseudo-scholarly books that purport to uncover the real and sensational historical facts behind the biblical story, or, more respectably, the current flourishing of historical Jesus research especially in America.[1] But there is an intriguing point about the latter. While rooted in modernism (with its naively objectivist view of history), it could be seen as hovering on the brink of postmodernism (with just the opposite view of history). The old criticism of the nineteenth-century quest of the historical Jesus—that its practitioners merely find the kind of Jesus they are looking for—could actually recommend the quest in postmodernist eyes. We may see the quest explicitly reformulating itself as the unfettered construction of the variety of Jesus figures a pluralist Christian culture needs. The future for unscholarly, frankly loony books about Jesus ought to be even brighter in the postmodern era.

2 My second and third points concern the way in which discussion of the authority of the Bible ought to respond to the modernist critique of authority. In the first place, within the Enlightenment's rejection of authority there was a necessary critique of authoritarianism, the coercive imposition of authority. The problem is that the way modernism formulated the opposition between freedom (autonomy) and authority made all forms of extrinsic authority seem to contradict freedom. All extrinsic authority seems authoritarian. If we are to distinguish the Bible's authority from authoritarianism, we need to think about authority and freedom in a different from that of modernism.

3 The crux of the problem of biblical authority in the context of modernism is the modernist prejudice against the particular and in favour of universal reason. But here postmodernism's critique of modernism turns the whole issue on its head, as we shall now see.

---

1 On this see further I Howard Marshall *Jesus at 2000* (Grove Biblical Series B 13, forthcoming September 1999).

3
The Postmodernist Rejection of Authority

There is a sense in which what postmodernism does is to take modernism's rejection of authority for the sake of autonomy to an extreme which subverts modernism. For postmodernists the modern project is itself authoritarian. Behind the Enlightenment's rhetoric of autonomy lies a project of domination.

What postmodernists recognize is that the tradition of Enlightenment thought is precisely a *particular tradition* of thought, like any other. Its claim to universality is the attempt to impose some people's particular perspective on others. It is part and parcel of the West's attempt to dominate the world, in which western science, technology and education are seen as equally applicable to any society, overriding and replacing indigenous cultural traditions. The purported universality of Enlightenment reason has been hand in glove with colonialism of all kinds, down to the degenerate economic and consumerist imperialism ('McWorld' as it has appropriately been called) which is dominant today. The story of the modern project is at least as much a story of domination as it is of enlightenment. The alleged progress of Enlightenment rationality has been an exercise of power.

Thus, in our terms, postmodernism extends the Enlightenment's rejection of authority not only to all extrinsic authority but also to the intrinsic authoritativeness of science and other forms of modern knowledge. The elitism which the modern exaltation of experts entails is the means by which some gain power over others. In other words, all pretensions to truth which others should accept, even when autonomous reason is supposed to be the criterion, are unmasked as means of domination. Hence, in postmodernism, freedom or autonomy comes to be opposed to every kind of authority, even the purported authority of truth. All truth is *somebody's* truth. I must be free to believe my own truth. The Enlightenment principle that there is no authority outside oneself is taken to its fullest possible extreme.

Thus, against Enlightenment universality, postmodernism celebrates particularity and diversity. The empowering of individuals and minority groups entails their epistemological autonomy over against the authoritarian claims of Enlightenment rationality. Groups and their traditions which have been marginalized and suppressed by the modern tradition receive affirmative action to reinstate them.

In principle postmodernism gives all groups and individuals the freedom and space to believe their own truths. But it does so by unmasking all beliefs as instruments in the struggle of diverse interest groups for power. In the pluralism of postmodern society there is no basis on which to argue or persuade. Stripping away the illusory pretensions of the Enlightenment to universal reason has left us with nothing but naked group self-interest and power politics. The roots of this may derive from a radical Marxist view of society, but it ends up with an intellectual world suspiciously like the unbridled capitalist free market with whose triumph it has coincided. Post-modernism, it seems, offers no realistic alternative to McWorld.

Because some people still think postmodernism is a rarefied intellectual game irrelevant to understanding our societies, let me illustrate its general cultural effects, which now seem to me blatantly clear at least in Britain and America. Modernists happily accepted their medical doctors' diagnoses and followed doctors' orders. Medicine was a major feature of the progress of Enlightenment reason. But the authority of modernist medicine and its experts has suffered remarkably in the last decade or so. More and more people are shopping around in a free market of alternative medicines. What modernist medicine pushed to the margins is increasingly coming in from the margins, and the choice between alternative forms of diagnosis and treatment is not made in the way modern rationality would require. It is just as much a judgment of preference as of reason. Alternative medicines profit from an image of the institutional structures of modernist medicine as structures of power which preserve the privileges of those who belong to them and exclude alternatives.

One could talk more generally also about the declining reputation of science, but let me bring us closer to home with a comment on postmodernist religion. In the modern period all religious authorities suffered a rationalist critique. Their claims could not pass the test of Enlightenment reason. At the popular level in this century the prestige of science was standardly pitted against religion, and in some ways that approach is still vigorous, as in the popular works of Richard Dawkins. But where postmodernist influences reach, scientism is waning. Postmodern people believe in all kinds of (by Enlightenment standards) irrational things—astrology, UFOs, crystals, reincarnation, and so on. But they reject any kind of authority beyond their free preference, which is often exercised in a pick-and-mix choice of seemingly (by modernist standards) incompatible elements. In hitherto secular northern Europe religious beliefs are resurgent (though 'religious' is a potentially misleading term here), but in a context in which talk of the authority of the Bible or of anything else is quite alien.

I said at the conclusion of the last section that the problem of biblical authority in the context of modernism is the modernist prejudice against the particular and in favour of universal reason. Postmodernism represents a radical reaction against universal reason in favour of the particular. In that sense, it may look more friendly to the biblical tradition. But postmodern relativism favours the particular only by reducing all truth claims to preference. To the authority of the Bible's claim to truth which is valid for all people postmodernism is probably even less hospitable than modernism.

4
The Authority of the Biblical Story

Too often we think of authority either in relation to commands or laws which we must obey or in relation to doctrines which we must believe. To some extent this is a legacy of the Enlightenment. But the Bible is not primarily a book of timeless doctrines or a book of moral laws. It is primarily a story. The one comprehensive category within which we can locate all the biblical materials is that of story, meaning the total biblical story of the world and God's purposes for it, stretching from creation to new creation. A key place within this overarching story is occupied by the gospel story of Jesus, but the gospel story is incomplete and lacks its fully biblical meaning apart from the more comprehensive story in which the Bible places it. The category of story includes not only biblical narratives—the many smaller narratives, many of them relatively self-contained, but canonically placed within the Bible's total story—but also prophecy and apostolic teaching insofar as these illuminate the meaning of the story and point its direction towards its still future completion. This total biblical story is also the context within which other biblical genres—law, prophecy, wisdom, psalms, ethical instruction, parables, and so on—are canonically placed. Story is the overarching category in which others are contextualized.

If we are to think of the Bible as authoritative, we must think primarily of the authority of this story. What does it mean to call this story authoritative? Postmodernism gives us a useful term here: metanarrative. (I shall come back to postmodernism's use of the term. For the moment we merely borrow the category.) The Bible's total story is a metanarrative. That is, it sketches in narrative form the meaning of all reality. To accept the authority of this story is to enter it and to inhabit it. It is to live in the world as the world is portrayed in this story. It is to let this story define our identity and our relationship to God and to others. It is to read the narratives of our own lives and of the societies in which we live as narratives which take their meaning from this metanarrative that overarches them all. To accept this metanarrative as the one within which we live is to see the world differently and to live within it differently from the way we would if we inhabited another metanarrative or framework of universal meaning.

The Bible's narrative does not simply require assent. Like all stories it draws us into its world, engages us imaginatively, allows us at our own pace to grow accustomed to it. But to accept it as authoritative metanarrative means more than to indwell it as we might a novel, imaginatively for the duration of our reading. Such an experience of a story may well affect our understanding and experience of the world. But to accept the Bible's metanarrative as authoritative is to privilege it above all other stories. It is to find our own identity as characters in that story, characters whose lives are an as yet untold part of the story. For the metanarrative is, of course, no more than a sketch. The Bible tells that part of the plot which makes the general meaning of the whole clear and points us ahead to the way the plot must be finally resolved. But it leaves the story open to the inclusion of all other stories, including those we play some part in writing.

For this reason it is important to stress that the biblical metanarrative remains unfinished. In the Bible its future conclusion is presented in general terms and in imaginative, not literal, depictions. This is necessary because we cannot find meaning in the rest of the story or discern God's intentions in the story as a whole without some knowledge of the conclusion to which God intends to bring it. But much that lies still on the way to that conclusion remains open. We ourselves play our part in writing the current chapter of the story, and for that purpose the overall biblical metanarrative functions authoritatively by setting the direction of the plot for us to follow. Understanding (to the degree the Bible allows us) the purposes of God in his world, we can align ourselves with those purposes and live in a way that anticipates their achievement.

The Particular and the Universal

This biblical metanarrative is the biblical way of combining particularity and universality. The metanarrative hinges on highly particular events—the history of Israel, the gospel story of Jesus—but reads these events as decisive for the meaning of the whole of reality. It links an imaginative sketch of the story of the whole world—from creation to the kingdom of God—with a highly particular story which is constitutive for the salvation of the world. The particularity is alien to modernism, the universality to postmodernism.

In a famous sentence the French philosopher Jean-François Lyotard defined the postmodern as 'incredulity towards metanarratives.'[2] At first sight it might seem that modernism was also incredulous of metanarratives. It rejected all religious myths which told a story of the meaning of the world. But in fact modernism created its own metanarrative: the idea of historical progress. Confidence in Enlightenment rationality was inseparable from the myth of enlightenment itself, the march of reason towards an ever more rational and better future. In the wake of the failure of this story, in both its progressivist and its Marxist revolutionary forms this century, postmodernism not only pronounces it incredible but unmasks it as a myth legitimating

---

2 J-F Lyotard, *The Postmodern Condition* (trans G Bennington and B Massumi; Minneapolis: University of Minnesota Press, 1984) p xxiv.

domination. The onward march of progress was the legitimation for suppressing difference and dissent. Generalizing from this exposure of the Enlightenment myth, postmodernism considers all metanarratives oppressive, since their claim to universal truth must be in reality the imposition of somebody's truth on others.

Freedom from Metanarratives?

Whether postmodernists themselves can or do live without any kind of metanarrative may be questioned. It is instructive to find that Friedrich Nietzsche, pioneer of postmodernism before its time, frequently embodies his sense of what it means to live after the death of God and after the death of the Enlightenment myth of progress in imaginative narratives. For example, he tells the parable of the three metamorphoses of the human spirit: the camel, the lion, and the child.[3] The camel is the weight-laden spirit, kneeling down to assume its burden and carrying its weight, the heavier the better, into the desert. The camel represents moral humanity, willingly taking on itself the burden of moral duty, to the point of asceticism. The lion, however, the next metamorphosis of the spirit, 'wants to capture freedom and to be lord.' It struggles for victory over the great dragon it no longer wishes to call 'lord' and God, the dragon that says 'Thou shalt.' The great dragon is called, 'Thou shalt,' but the lion says 'I will.' The victory of the lion means no more 'Thou shalt,' only 'I will.' The lion is needed to create freedom for the human spirit, freedom from given values, freedom to create its own values. But the actual creation of new values lies not with the lion, but with the child who is the third and last metamorphosis. The child is a new beginning, humanity as truly self-created. 'The spirit now wills *its own* will. The spirit sundered from the world now wins *its own* world.' The child is the superman, whose will is absolute, who creates his own values, his own world. The parable is a metanarrative which presumably escapes the charge of totalizing oppression by leading not to predetermined closure, but to the absolute freedom from constraint, the freedom to make one's own world, that the postmodern spirit craves. If such a metanarrative escapes the postmodern incredulity towards all grand stories, it is worth asking whether a Christian alternative, just as alive to the issues of authority, obedience and freedom, but construing their nature and relationships differently, may likewise, in its own terms, escape the charge of totalizing oppression. In the next section we shall suggest the way in which this could be done.

The case for the Christian metanarrative is not helped by the way it became entwined with the modern myth of progress in the nineteenth century.

---

[3] F Nietzsche, *Thus Spoke Zarathrustra*, tr R J Hollingdale (London: Penguin, 1969) pp 54–56.

But the abject failure of that alliance with modernism should warn us against too easy an alliance with postmodernism, reducing the biblical narrative to no more than the story we Christians choose to tell about ourselves, an unpretentious local fiction without truth claims. The challenge of postmodernism is to show how the biblical metanarrative liberates rather than oppresses. Is it a story which must suppress all others or a story which in some sense holds open space for all others?

Freedom and Mastery

The modernist metanarrative of progress was a narrative of mastery. Enlightenment reason was always essentially aimed at mastering the world through knowledge in order to master it by technology. Autonomous reason in thought aimed at implementing and securing human freedom in the world, that is, the freedom of the master who subjects the slave to his will. The project was to subject the world to human will in order to remake it according to human desires. Increasingly the future would be subjected to human control. It is not surprising that this myth of progress through human domination of the rest of creation entailed also progress through the domination of some humans over others.

The myth lives on in such increasingly dangerous forms as bioengineering. It is noteworthy, once again, that postmodernism, while it unmasks the myth of the Enlightenment, offers no real resistance to its effects. The reason is that postmodernism itself represents a further step along the line of thinking in which freedom or autonomy entails mastery. The modernist mastered the world through science and technology, the postmodernist constructs it textually. Retreating into a purely linguistic world of arbitrary signs, the postmodernist gains freedom from all authority, but leaves the modernist free to continue subjecting the extra-linguistic world to abuse.

The problem caused by the Enlightenment's concept of autonomy as freedom from all extrinsic authority is not solved by pushing further in the same direction, as postmodernism does. In this light we can see that the biblical metanarrative offers not another legitimation of domination, but a genuine alternative. This metanarrative, by placing the future in God's hands, liberates us from the need for mastery or control, restoring to us a properly human way of living in relationship with the rest of reality, neither subjecting it to our will nor constructing it at will. This depends on recognizing the kind of authority the metanarrative attributes to God as the authority of grace.

5
The Authority of Grace

The biblical metanarrative is a story not of the assertion of autonomy against domination, but of grace and free response. In this story all is given by God, including freedom. The world, our being in it, our redemption from the evil we make of it—all are God's gift, which always precedes God's requirements of us. This is part of the significance of the fact that law and commands in the Bible are contextualized within its narrative. Authority belongs in the first place to the story of God's gracious self-giving to us. In that context the authority of his will for us expressed in commands is the authority of his grace. Another way of putting this is to appeal to the biblical notion of covenant. In the context of the covenant relationship, God's commands are not abstract norms, but the obligations of a relationship into which God's self-giving generosity has invited us. To God's gift and promise, his covenant partners respond with gratitude and glad trust. To obey his commands is to take part, as his covenant partners, in God's redeeming and fulfilling intentions for his creation. Seen from the context of the covenant relationship of grace, God's commands are not coercive and repressive, but liberating and empowering.

Thus our response to grace is not the constrained submission of the slave, but the free obedience of love. Its paradigm is: 'I delight to do your will, O my God; your law is within my heart' (Ps 40.8). This is neither the autonomy that is contradicted by any authority nor the heteronomy that experiences authority as alien subjection to the will of another. It is the obedience to God of those who already glimpse the eschatological identity of their best desires with God's, who recognize God's will as the desire of their own hearts, whose experience of God's love makes love the freely chosen goal of their lives. Freedom is here not the rejection of all limits, but the free acceptance of those limits which enable loving relationships. Obedience is demanding, but it is no more heteronomous than the athlete's acceptance of the demanding regime that she knows to be the way to the goals she has set herself. For those who make God their goal, the wholehearted obedience, extending to the whole of life, which is required of them is gladly and freely undertaken as the way along which they find at every step of obedience the God they seek: 'With my whole heart I seek you; do not let me stray from your commandments' (Ps 119.26). (A postmodernist critique at this point would consist in an appeal to diversity: there are an indefinite variety of life-goals one may choose, and to pronounce one better than others is impose one's own choice on others. But this, as so often turns out to be the case with postmodernism, is the philosophy of consumerism, which exalts choice as the supreme value in itself, irrespective of the content of choice. It has been suggested that the real metanarrative by which our contemporary western society lives, and to which postmodernism contributes, is the late capitalist economic myth in which consumerism plays a central role.[4])

Because obedience to God, whose will is the true law of my own being, is different in kind from obedience to human authorities, the biblical writers struggle with analogies for it. The analogy of servants' or slaves' obedience to their master or subjects' obedience to their king is frequent, but is also transmuted by paradox: 'As slaves of God, live as free people' (1 Pet 2.16); 'the perfect law, the law of liberty' (Jas 1.25). In John 15.14–15 Jesus says: 'You are my friends if you do what I command you. I do not call you servants any longer, because the servant does not know what the master is doing; but I have called you friends, because I have made known to you everything that I have heard from my Father.' What Jesus here drops from the image of servants is not the language of command and obedience ('You are my friends if you do what I *command* you'!), but the requirement of *blind* obedience which is made of the mere slave. Like Jesus himself in obedience to his Father, his friends know what is the aim his commandments have in view, and themselves accept that aim.

But within the relationship of grace, which enables this kind of enlightened obedience to God's will, there remain, while we still live by faith, occasions for obedience in sheer faith without understanding. Jesus, who obeyed his Father's will in perfect understanding of it (such that the paradigm of Ps 40.8 applies pre-eminently to him, as Hebrews 10.5–7 recognizes), is the limit-case on the one side. Abraham on mount Moriah (Gen 22.1–14) is the limit-case on the other side. Although he was the friend of God (Isa 40.8) to whom God made known his purposes (Gen 18.17–19), Abraham had to obey the command to sacrifice Isaac in completely uncomprehending trust. The command to sacrifice of Isaac unavoidably causes offence to modernist and postmodernist outlooks alike. Yet even this episode is not the subjection to heteronomy it would be if it stood alone, outside the context of the wider story of Abraham and the wider story of the Bible. In context it is obedience to the God who, the story of his grace shows, can be trusted in spite of appearances. Abraham's obedience is the measure of the extent to which he has made this gracious God's will the desire of his own heart. While we rightly experience, in reading the story, the conflict of autonomy and heteronomy which we all know, in its wider context the story points us beyond this conflict. Both it and its polar opposite, the obedience of Jesus as the alternative limit-case, point to the eschatological goal beyond autonomy and heteronomy, the final identity of human freedom and divine authority.

---

4 See further the exploration of postmodernity and consumerism in Graham Cray, *Postmodern Culture and Youth Discipleship* (Grove Pastoral Series P 76, 1998).

6
Story, Commands and Doctrines

The Bible's authority inheres, we have argued, primarily in the metanarrative —the most inclusive way of characterizing the Bible's content. We acknowledge this authority as we inhabit the narrative and relate to God and the world as we find them portrayed in this narrative. What then of the authority of commands and doctrines, with which we more commonly associate the term 'authority'?

We have already shown to some degree the importance of the location of biblical laws and commands within the narrative of God's grace. It is from this narrative that we 'know what God is doing,' such that our obedience, in Johannine terms, transcends the blind obedience of the servant and resembles the understanding obedience of the son, the daughter or the friend. That biblical commands are not arbitrary decrees but correspond to the way the world is and will be is fully appreciable only as we inhabit the Bible's narrative and appropriate its perspective on how the world is and will be. The point is important because it will by no means necessarily be evident within the worldviews of our society that biblical commands correspond to the way the world is. Theories of natural law which attempt to demonstrate this independently of the biblical narrative have a certain value, but they are never completely successful, and in a postmodern society are unlikely to carry much conviction at all. Recognizing the importance of the biblical metanarrative enables us to see that inhabiting it is learning to see the world significantly differently (though not of course in every respect differently) from the way the cultural traditions of our context see it. Biblical laws which 'make no sense' in relation to the world as those traditions portray it may do so in relation to the world as the biblical story portrays it.

However, there is another important point to make about biblical commands. An obvious problem about the authority of biblical commands is that there are a very large number of such commands which Christians recognize no obligation to obey. The following are some examples selected to illustrate the diversity of such commands (I include more NT than OT examples in order to forestall an obvious but unsatisfactory response to the problem).

> You shall not eat flesh with its blood (Gen 9.4).
> Do not be too righteous and do not act too wisely (Eccles 7.16).
> You shall not sow your field with two kinds of seed, nor shall you put on a garment made of two different materials (Lev 19.19).

Greet one another with a holy kiss (1 Thes 5.26).
Do not adorn yourselves outwardly by braiding your hair (1 Pet 3.3, addressed to women).
Let a widow be put on the list if she is not less than sixty years old and has been married only once (1 Tim 5.9).
Anyone who is unwilling to work should not eat (2 Thes 3.10).
Slaves, obey your earthly masters with fear and trembling (Eph 6.5).
If anyone will not welcome you or listen to your words, shake off the dust from your feet as you leave that house or town (Matt 10.4).
Give to everyone who begs from you (Luke 6.30).

Christians turn out to be very selective about which biblical commands they consider themselves obliged to obey—or at least to obey literally. Are they therefore recognizing no authority in these commands? The problem with an approach to biblical authority which emphasizes authoritative commands apart from the biblical story is that it must simply ignore these many commands which do not seem to oblige us to obey them. If, however, they are read within their context in the biblical story, then the story defines their authority contextually. This approach enables us to learn from commands which we do not think require our literal obedience. Their place in the story may delimit or relativize their authority as commands. They may not be instructions addressed to us, but they can still be instructive for us.

Too Many...or Too Few?

A different, though not unrelated, problem frequently encountered in respect to biblical commands is that on many aspects of life where we would expect an authoritative Scripture to guide our decision making and practice, the Bible simply does not—however hard the interpreters try to make it—speak with a single clear voice. On war and peace, on the relationships of men and women, on slavery, on the ethics of material possessions, and a host of other issues of great importance for living in obedience to God, the Bible contains a disturbing diversity of statements and approaches, including various commands and instructions as well as narrative examples and wisdom reflections. Unless we are to pick and choose arbitrarily among these relevant biblical materials, we need a perspective in which the diversity acquires an intelligible shape, in which, one might say, a *direction* of biblical teaching becomes apparent and the texts can be read dynamically, as pointing us in that direction, even though some go less far in that direction than others.[5] Such an approach makes sense in the context of our recognition that

---

5 For the hermeneutical principle of discerning the *direction* of biblical thought, see R Bauckham, *The Bible in Politics: How to Read the Bible Politically* (London: SPCK, 1989) p 103; and for a worked example, see R Bauckham, 'Egalitarianism and Hierarchy in the

it is as a metanarrative that the Bible is authoritative, not exclusively but primarily. A biblical approach to an issue may then be expected to emerge in the course of the story, taking shape as we observe different aspects of such an approach appearing in different contexts, and even as we take account of a variety of approaches that, on an obvious reading, might seem contradictory. What might seem, when one text is read alone, to be that text's straightforward answer to a question we are asking might have to be relativized by other perspectives on the matter given us by other texts. All this may seem a frustratingly oblique way of providing us with the teaching we seek to live by, but we can come to appreciate its advantages when we read the Bible in such a way as to let it involve us in its story and in the dynamism of the way God's will for his people and for the world comes to be known. In discerning the direction in the diversity we come to a richer understanding of an issue and its outworking in the diversity of historical human life than a single straightforward pronouncement could afford us.

If the problem of looking in the Bible for authoritative commands is that there appear to be far too many of them, then the problem of looking in the Bible for authoritative doctrines is that there appear to be far too few of them. But this is because, once again, it is the story that is primary, such that the Bible's theological teaching about who God is and who we are in relation to God and the world is inseparable from the story of God and the world which it tells. This is why, for example, the Bible both does and does not teach the doctrine of the Trinity. Even though I think the New Testament more explicitly trinitarian than most New Testament scholars do, still the New Testament does not provide explicit confessions of the trinitarian being of God in himself. But the story of God's acting and suffering in the world in the gospel story of Jesus is trinitarian in form. That God is trinitarian emerges, as it were, from the story. A doctrine of the Trinity represents what we need to say about God in himself for the biblical story about God to be a true story. It is authorized by the story in that it follows from taking the story seriously as authoritative metanarrative. Neither what the Bible obliges us to believe nor what the Bible obliges us to do can be known from isolated texts, but requires their total context in the biblical metanarrative.

Biblical Traditions,' in A N S Lane (ed), *Interpreting the Bible: Historical and Theological Studies in honour of David F Wright* (Leicester: Apollos, 1997) pp 259–273.

7
Other Modes of Authority

Once we begin to explore the great variety of kinds of literature that the Bible contains, we must come to realize that the sense in which we can attribute authority to Scripture must vary considerably according to the kind of content we find in the various biblical books and passages. It is not only narrative that escapes our habitual thinking about authority in terms of commands and doctrines.

In the wisdom literature, for example, it will not do to treat the aphorisms in Proverbs as divine commands to be obeyed or the wise reflection on experience of life in Ecclesiastes as doctrine to be believed. It might be more appropriate to formulate the authority attaching to such inspired thoughtfulness as the authority to recommend, 'Think about this!' While commandments are formed to be obeyed, aphorisms are formed to be savoured and pondered.

In the case of the Psalms, again, neither commandment nor doctrine is an appropriate model. As Israel's temple hymn-book, the authoritative recommendation with which they come is, most generally, 'This is how you should pray; make use of these vehicles of prayer for every occasion.' But in some cases, it might be better understood as, 'You can even say that to God!' The imprecatory or other difficult psalms, so problematic if we attribute an inappropriate mode of authority to them, come into their own as soon as we see that their authority is such as to give us permission to be honest with God, to bring all our concerns to God and to let God deal with them. For some psalms, the authoritative recommendation must surely be, 'Join in this so that you may learn experientially to appreciate and to praise God!' Theirs is an authority to enable worship and to empower us to join creation's praise.

Fictional stories, such as Jesus' parables or (as I take it to be) the book of Jonah do not have the authority of historical reports, but that of appeal to the imagination so as to change our perspective on things. The way such stories creep up on us and make their point by taking us unawares, or the way they use humour to startle us out of familiar ways of thinking, do not fit any conventional notion of authority at all. They ask only to be heard by those willing to open the ears of their imagination.

While we often think of authority as obliging us, it is also possible to think of authority as *authorizing* us. There are many ways in which we can apply such a notion within the varieties of biblical literature. Gospel stories of people like ourselves coming to Jesus with their needs or their questions *authorize* us to do the same. A command such as the great commission at the end of Matthew's Gospel *authorizes* us to act with the delegated authority of the Lord Jesus in making disciples of all nations for the kingdom of God. Much that we often think of as obedience can also be construed as being authorized, a construal that may restore to our thinking the sense of privilege and responsibility that often attaches in biblical thought to the vocabulary of obedience. More generally, the way the Bible speaks of God—which, since God is the transcendent and incomprehensible one, beyond all our language and categories of thought, should never be taken for granted, but received as a constant source of amazement and gratitude—*authorizes* us to do what we should never otherwise think ourselves able to do: to speak of God. There is much more that would bear exploration along these lines.

8
Authority and Freedom in Biblical Interpretation

It is potentially disastrous to speak of the authority of the Bible without also raising hermeneutical questions. It has been a not uncommon phenomenon in the history of interpretation for biblical authority to be used to authorize whatever views the interpreters have wanted to Bible to express. At worst the Bible has in this way been abused as an ideological tool of self-interest and domination. Yet a certain degree of freedom in interpretation is inescapable. We need to see how this can serve rather than subvert the authority of the Bible.

Insofar as biblical scholarship until recently was concerned with the meaning of the text, rather than with historical reconstruction behind the text, its efforts were directed to establishing the 'original' meaning. This is often defined as the meaning intended by the original author, though it would be better defined as the meaning which the first readers could be expected to find in the text (since authors can fail to express what they really mean and can entertain private meanings inaccessible to any reader). The historical scholarship deployed in this task is a form of Enlightenment rationality. This is not a reason to denigrate it; its achievement has been massive and no responsible hermeneutic can leave it aside. It had, however, limitations typical of Enlightenment thinking. It ignored the perspective of the interpreter, giving the illusion of complete objectivity. It therefore pursued the expectation that disinterested scholarship could achieve agreement on the one and only original meaning of the text. The aim was to specify the historical meaning of the text as precisely as possible, thereby identifying 'an immovable textual basis for Christian existence.'[6] This attempt to pin down, as it were, once and for all the meaning of the text looks suspiciously like an attempt to master and to control the text.

Despite its enormous achievements, in its ultimate aim this pursuit of the original meaning (now continued also with new methods, such as social scientific methods) has failed. Rather than achieving a consensus, the nature of this scholarly enterprise seems perpetually to incite new interpretations and unending interpretative debates. There is real progress, but not as much as many practitioners like to think. Moreover, the aim of establishing a secure meaning to which the Bible's authority for faith and practice can be attached is frustrated by the plurality of original meanings propounded. Worse still, very often the more precisely the meaning of the text for its original readers in their precise historical context is specified, the less relevance the text appears to have for any other readers.

Postmodern reading is altogether different. From the naive historical objectivism of modernist reading postmodernist readers are freed to create meaning for themselves. The text is explicitly subjected to the reader's authority.

Thus in modernist reading the attempt to tie the text's meaning down to the one original reading determined by the interpreter effectively controls the text by disallowing any fresh meaning it may acquire in other contexts. An historical reconstruction of the original meaning replaces the text. In postmodernist reading the text's meaning is not tied down but opened up to as many interpretations as there are readers. Here it is readers' creation of meaning which replaces the text. In neither case can the text itself speak with authority to a contemporary context.

Locating Meaning

For this to be seen as possible, we must recognize that meaning does not simply reside in the text (as it does for modernist reading) nor is it simply created by readers (as it is in postmodernist reading). It happens in interaction between the text itself and its readers. Readers encounter the text as genuinely other than themselves. Historical exegesis helps them to perceive this other, but its otherness is not limited to its historical meaning. Reading the text not only with disciplined historical imagination but also with the prejudices and the concerns of their own contexts, readers experience it as speaking to those contexts. In a sense, this gives space for the freedom of readers in interpretation. They are free to bring their own perspectives to the

---

6 T A Hart, *Faith Thinking: The Dynamics of Christian Theology* (London: SPCK, 1995/Downers Grove: Inter-Varsity Press, 1996) p 119.

text. But the same space which allows such freedom to readers also allows the text the freedom to transcend its original historical context and to mean what it can mean to other contexts. Indeed, in such fresh occurrence of meaning God himself is free to speak his word with authority.

In summary, this is a hermeneutic which requires the interpreter seriously to listen to the text and to do so as someone who listens, not in abstraction from her own context, but in deliberate awareness of her own context. It is the listening that allows the text to speak with authority and the context that allows the text to speak with relevance.

Of course, in the church individuals do not come to the text in isolation from the community, nor do they read the text as though it had never been interpreted before. Interpretation should normally be the activity of the community, in which individuals play various specific parts, and it should normally be in recognizable continuity with the tradition. These dimensions help interpretation to avoid the idiosyncrasy to which the hermeneutic we have described could be subject were it practised by individuals apart from the tradition and the life of the church. But there is an important qualification. Scripture may speak freshly to a lone individual or a marginal group in a way that challenges tradition and community and in a way that the church is initially unwilling to hear. We must allow for the Jeremiahs and the Luthers.

Reading and Listening

Recognizing the Bible's authority entails in the first place listening. Although the Bible insists that hearing without doing is worthless (Matt 7.24–27; Jas 1.22–25; Rev 1.3), it also insists that the hearing that leads to practice must be attentive listening: 'Let anyone with ears to hear listen!' (Mark 4.9 and elsewhere); 'Let anyone who has an ear listen to what the Spirit says to the churches' (Rev 2.7 and elsewhere). Fundamental to the Bible's authority is this claim to be heard as a matter both of urgency and of continuing attention. It is attentive and extended listening to the text that both the modern and the postmodern approaches to interpretation tend to impede, but which the practices of reading of Scripture in the context of the life of the church have usually endeavoured to promote. While postmodern reading hastens to make meaning of its own out of the text and cannot wait for the text itself to yield meaning, modern reading sees the task of interpretation as done once it has pinned down the original meaning once and for all—or at least until the next historical critic proposes a rival meaning. Attentive listening, on the other hand, remains open to the unlimited possibilities of meaning which can occur: 'We must return to the text again and again and submit our interpretations to it, never resting content that we have the meaning pinned down for good. If we fall into the latter trap we cease to be faithful in our submission to the authority of Scripture as such, and exalt our best readings of it instead.'[7] Practices of attentive listening have also helped the church to avoid the kind of entrenched traditionalism that merely repeats in the present what was said in the past in the way that it was said in the past. For the attentive listener, the Bible's authoritative voice does not come only from the past, but is a living voice in the present calling us into the future.

Serious listening entails dialogue, in which the listener interrogates the text and the text interrogates the listener. Such a process brings all kinds of aspects of the attentive listener's context into relationship to the text in order to discover how to live within the biblical metanarrative at precisely its present juncture. Here it is perhaps important to use the image of inhabiting the world of the biblical story with some care. It does not mean living in a purely textual world unrelated to the contemporary world in which others live. Rather, by living within the biblical story we can construe our contemporary world in the unique configuration it has when viewed as the world that must become what it will in the final purpose of God.

The *unfinished* nature of the biblical story—or, more positively, the eschatological hope as the ultimate future God will give to his world—is what creates the space for finding ourselves and our contemporary world in the biblical story. It is what enables and requires the hermeneutic of listening in context that we have briefly suggested. It is what resists the premature closure that would stifle the freedom of obedient Christian living in the contemporary world. It is what both keeps the story open to the inclusion of all other stories and invites all other stories to find the ending that will give them meaning in the coming kingdom of God. Properly to grasp the way the authority of the biblical text and the freedom of ecclesial interpreters relate without contradiction, we must appeal not just to general hermeneutical principles, but to the nature of the metanarrative in which the Bible's authority primarily inheres.

---

[7] Hart, *Faith Thinking*, p 142.

9
Bibliography

The works to which I am most conscious of being indebted in this booklet are:

W Brueggemann, 'The Commandments and Liberated, Liberating Bonding,' in *Interpretation and Obedience* (Minneapolis: Fortress, 1991) pp 145–158.
J Goldingay, *Models for Scripture* (Grand Rapids: Eerdmans/Carlisle: Paternoster, 1994).
C Gunton, *Enlightenment and Alienation* (Basingstoke: Marshall Morgan & Scott, 1985).
T A Hart, *Faith Thinking: The Dynamics of Christian Theology* (London: SPCK, 1995/Downers Grove: Inter-Varsity Press, 1996).
T A Hart, '(Probably) the Greatest Story Ever Told? Reflections on Brueggemann's *The Bible and Postmodern Imagination*,' in A N S Lane (ed), *Interpreting the Bible: Historical and Theological Studies in Honour of David F Wright* (Leicester: Apollos, 1997) pp 181–204.
N Lash, *Voices of Authority* (London: Sheed & Ward, 1976).
J R Middleton and B J Walsh, *Truth Is Stranger Than It Used to Be: Biblical Faith in a Postmodern Age* (Downers Grove: Inter-Varsity Press, 1995).
A C Thiselton, 'Authority and Hermeneutics: Some Proposals for a More Creative Agenda,' in P E Satterthwaite and D F Wright (eds), *A Pathway into the Holy Scripture* (Grand Rapids: Eerdmans, 1994) pp 107–141.

See also:

R Bauckham, 'Tradition in relation to Scripture and Reason,' in B Drewery and R Bauckham (eds), *Scripture Tradition and Reason: A Study in the Criteria of Christian Doctrine* (R P C Hanson FS; Edinburgh: T & T Clark, 1988) pp 117–145.